# SHARE YOUR PARAGRAPH

*An Interactive Process Approach to Writing*

# SHARE YOUR PARAGRAPH

## An Interactive Process Approach to Writing

**George Rooks**

*University of California–Davis*

**PRENTICE HALL REGENTS**

*Englewood Cliffs, New Jersey 07632*

*Library of Congress Cataloging-in-Publication Data*

Rooks, George.
  Share your paragraph.

  1. English language—Paragraphs.  2. English
language—Text-books for foreign speakers.  I.  Title.
PE1439.R66  1988        428.2'4        87–7356
ISBN 0–13–808271–5

Cover design: Photo Plus Art
Manufacturing buyer: Margaret Rizzi
Photo research: Kay Dellosa

Photo credits (by paragraph number): (1) Ken Karp. (2) UN Photo 149097
by John Isaac. (3) George Rooks. (4) Laimute E. Druskis. (5) Trans World
Airlines. (6) George Rooks. (7) Marc P. Anderson. (8) Laimute E. Druskis.
(9) Volkswagen of America. (10) George Rooks. (11) UN Photo 153916 by
Doranne Jacobson. (12) United Nations. (13) National Center for Atmo-
spheric Research/National Science Foundation. (14) The Port of New York
Authority. (15) FDA. (16) Sugarbush Valley Ski Resort. (17) Action. (18)
Prentice Hall Photo Archives. (19) George Rooks. (20) Eugene Gordon.

©1988 by Prentice-Hall, Inc.
A Division of Simon & Schuster
Englewood Cliffs, New Jersey 07632

Printed in the United States of America
10  9  8  7  6  5  4  3  2  1

ISBN 0-13-808271-5        01

Prentice-Hall International (UK) Limited, *London*
Prentice-Hall of Australia Pty. Limited, *Sydney*
Prentice-Hall Canada Inc., *Toronto*
Prentice-Hall Hispanoamericana, S.A., *Mexico*
Prentice-Hall of India Private Limited, *New Delhi*
Prentice-Hall of Japan, Inc., *Tokyo*
Simon & Schuster Asia Pte. Ltd., *Singapore*
Editora Prentice-Hall do Brasil, Ltda., *Rio de Janeiro*

*I dedicate this book to my wife, Hila,*
*for her unending inspiration, love, and support.*

# CONTENTS

# PREFACE

*Share Your Paragraph* is for high beginning and low intermediate ESL students. Despite the title, paragraph structure is not the primary concern of this book, even though such structure is implicitly emphasized by each paragraph in the Prewriting and Editing sections.

Instead, the primary purpose of this book is twofold: (1) to provide the ESL student with a provocative approach to writing; (2) to provide a setting in which *students' own writing is the central focus of the writing class.*

To achieve this twofold purpose, a process approach to paragraph writing is used. Each unit has five parts: Prewriting, Writing, Sharing, Revising, and Editing. In the *Prewriting* section, students are asked to read and analyze a sample paragraph. Then, after discussing their ideas with their classmates, the students are asked to cluster their own ideas about the assigned topic. In the *Writing* section, the student transforms his or her cluster into sentence-paragraph form, concentrating on ideas, not grammar. The *Sharing* section then calls for the student to exchange what has been written so far with one or more classmates. Next, the student *revises* the paragraph, using the ideas gained from other class members. Finally, in the *Editing* section, the student is asked to complete some exercises that have relevance to the topic at hand. Then, after the student has edited his or her own paragraph, it is submitted to the teacher for evaluation.

Secondarily, this book is organized according to verb tenses. It is meant to be used in conjunction with, or to complement, the grammar class. The Editing section of each unit is devoted to work in such areas as verbs, pro-nouns, prepositions, articles, adjectives, compound sen-tences, subordinate clauses, and relative clauses. Particular attention is paid to punctuation and capitalization. Of course, the teacher is encouraged to bring supplemental material to class as she or he feels is appropriate. Neverthe-less, the author feels strongly that such material, as well as the exercises in the Editing section, should be of secondary importance. After all, writing is more than grammar; it is communication.

As always, flexibility is crucial. Every class is different, as is every teacher. Ultimately, this book seeks to provide a lucid, stimulating introduction to writing for the student and an enjoyable resource for the teacher.

# TO THE TEACHER

There are twenty paragraph units. It is suggested that each unit consume four to five hours of class time as follows:

**Hours 1–2** Discussion of the photograph on the first page of the unit (see the Instructor's Manual for preparagraph discussion suggestions); discussion of the paragraph in the Prewriting section (and accompanying exercise); clustering of ideas; completion of Writing section

**Hour 3** Completion of the Sharing and Revising sections

**Hour 4** Completion of the Editing section, and production of the final edited version of the paragraph

**Hour 5** Discussion of, and comparison of, paragraphs produced—with possible final revision and editing based on teacher's comments and evaluation

General notes:

1. Discussion of the paragraph in the Prewriting section should include an extensive discussion of vocabulary contained therein as well as vocabulary that might be used in the students' paragraphs.
2. Students have a tendency to want to rush through the Sharing and Revising sections. Teachers should stress the value of these activities, and should encourage students to proceed slowly and thoughtfully.
3. The students' final editing (before teacher evaluation) should be done with an eye toward remedying problems

evidenced in previous writing. This focus should be provided by the teacher.

4. There is no substitute for comparison of student writing. If possible, the teacher should make copies of at least three or four paragraphs per unit and distribute them for class discussion.

# SHARE YOUR PARAGRAPH

*An Interactive Process Approach
to Writing*

# PARAGRAPH
# 1

*Write about yourself.*

## PREWRITING

Read and discuss the following paragraph about Oscar Alvarado with your class. What ideas does Oscar Alvarado communicate to you? What do you think about Oscar?

I am Oscar Alvarado. I am 21 years old. I am a little fat, but I am very handsome! I am 1.72 meters tall, and my weight is 80 kg. My hair is black and long. My blue eyes are beautiful. I am a Venezuelan. I am from Caracas. In Caracas, I am an engineering student at Bolívar University, the best university in Venezuela. Now I am an English student in the United States. I am happy here, but I miss my girlfriends, Carolina, Marilia, and Marta, very much!

The following drawing is a cluster. Oscar Alvarado made it before he wrote the paragraph. Fill in the empty places in the cluster with information from the paragraph. Which information is not in the paragraph?

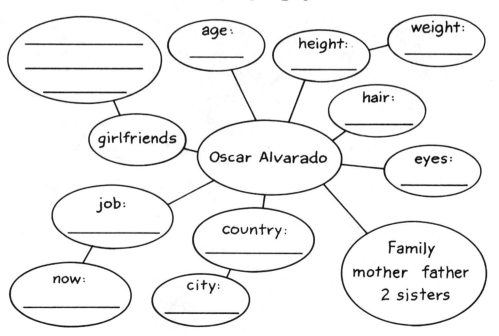

Now think about yourself. What would you like to communicate about yourself? What do you think of when you think of yourself? Make a big cluster about yourself.

## WRITING

Now use your cluster to write a paragraph about yourself. This paragraph is *not* for your teacher. It is for you to share with your classmates. Don't worry about grammar at this point; feel free to make changes as you write.

_____

_____

_____

_____

_____

_____

_____

_____

_____

_____

_____

_____

_____

_____

_____

## SHARING

Read your paragraph to a small group of your classmates or to one of your classmates (you may read it more than once, and you may give it to them to read). Ask them what they think about your paragraph. Do they understand everything? Is there anything they don't understand? Ask them for at least one more piece of information that they would like to see in your paragraph.

After you hear from your classmates, read your paragraph again. Is there anything you want to change? How can you communicate your ideas more clearly?

## REVISING

Rewrite your paragraph. Change anything you want. You may change words, phrases, sentences, or the whole paragraph. You may add, subtract, or reorder. Study the following example. Oscar Alvarado wrote it *before* he wrote the paragraph on page 2. Look back at that paragraph. What changes did Oscar make? Why did he make them? What did he add, subtract, and reorder?

My name is Oscar Alvarado. Now I am an English student in the United States. I am a Venezuelan. I am from Caracas. My father is a lawyer in Caracas. In Caracas, I am a student at Bolívar University. I am 21 years old. I am fat, but I am handsome. I am 1.72 meters tall, and my weight is 80 kg. My hair is black and long. My blue eyes are beautiful. I miss my girlfriends, Carolina, Marilia, and Marta, very much!

Now revise your paragraph.

_____

_____

_____

_____

_____

_____

_____

_____

_____

_____

_____

_____

_____

_____

## EDITING

Now is the time to pay attention to the grammar in your paragraph. Study the following exercises and complete them. Think about them in connection with your paragraph. When you finish the exercises, edit your paragraph. If necessary, make changes in grammar, punctuation, word order, and any other item; then give it to your teacher.

## Exercise A.  Present-tense verbs

*Directions:*  Put in **am, is,** or **are.**

My name _____ Ling-Chen Chu. I _____ a Chinese student
                $1$                         $2$
from the People's Republic of China. I _____ from Shanghai. I
                                              $3$
_____ a secondary school physics teacher in Beijing. I _____
   $4$                                                            $5$
married. My husband _____ an elementary school English
                          $6$
teacher. We have one daughter. Her name _____ Ruey-ling. I
                                                 $7$
_____ 27 years old. I _____ short and thin. My hair and my
   $8$                       $9$
eyes _____ black. I don't think that my appearance _____
        $10$                                               $11$
important.

## Exercise B.  Punctuation and capitalization

*Directions:*   Statements start with a **capital letter** and end with
                a **period.** Add punctuation to the following paragraph and correct the capitalization.

*Example:*  I am Oscar Alvarado.

   i am Oscar Alvarado   i am 21 years old   i am a little fat, but
i am very handsome   i am 1.72 meters tall, and my weight
is 80 kg   my hair is black and long   my blue eyes are
beautiful   i am a Venezuelan   i am from Caracas   in Caracas, i am an engineering student at Bolívar University, the best

university in Venezuela   now i am an English student in the
United States   i am happy here, but i miss my girlfriends, Carolina, Marilia, and Marta, very much

## Exercise C.  Sentence order

> *Directions:*   Place the words in the right order. Be sure to put a
> capital letter at the beginning of each sentence
> and a period at the end of the sentence. Some
> items may have more than one possible order.

1.  am, I, 27, old, years

    *I am 27 years old.*_____

2.  student, am, Chinese, I, a

    _____

3.  elementary, teacher, my, school, is, an, husband, English

    _____

4.  eyes, black, and, are, my, hair, my

    _____

5.  and, I, short, thin, am

    _____

6.  People's, a, I, the, from, of, Chinese, China, Republic, am,
    student

    _____

7.  from, I, Shanghai, am

    _____

8.  Beijing, in, teacher, physics, school, secondary, a, am, I

    _____

# PARAGRAPH
## 2

*Write about your father.*

## PREWRITING

Read and discuss the following paragraph about Mr. Tamimi with your class. The paragraph was written by Mr. Tamimi's daughter Khadija. How does Khadija feel about her father? How does she communicate her ideas and feelings?

My father is Mohammed Al-Tamimi. He is about 50 years old. He is tall and thin. I don't know exactly how tall he is, and I don't know how much he weighs. He has black hair, a moustache, and a goatee. He is a car dealer in Riyadh, Saudi Arabia. He sells Mercedes Benz and Porsche cars. His company is large. More than 50 people work for him. My father is very smart. I love my father, but I don't see him a lot. Usually he is at his company or with my brothers. I think that he is the best father in the world to his fifteen children.

Khadija made the following cluster when she was thinking about her father. Fill in the empty places in the cluster. Look at the information she did *not* use. Why do you think she didn't use some of the information?

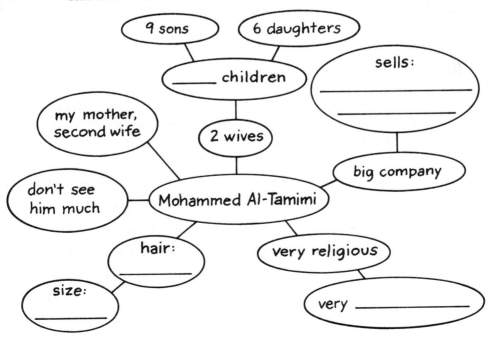

Think about your father. What feelings and ideas come into your mind? Make a cluster about him.

## WRITING

Use the cluster to write a paragraph about your father. You don't have to use the entire cluster, and you may add information not in the cluster. Remember, this is not for your teacher. It is for you to share with your classmates.

_____

_____

_____

_____

_____

_____

_____

_____

_____

_____

_____

_____

_____

_____

## SHARING

Read your paragraph to a small group of your classmates or to one of your classmates (you may read it more than once, and you may give it to them to read). Ask them what they think about your paragraph. Do they understand everything? Is there anything they don't understand? Ask them for at least one more piece of information that they would like to see in your paragraph.

After you hear from your classmates, read your paragraph again. Decide what you want to change. How can you communicate your ideas more clearly?

## REVISING

Rewrite your paragraph. Change anything you want. You may change words, phrases, sentences, or the whole paragraph. You may add, subtract, or reorder.

_____

_____

_____

_____

_____

_____

_____

_____

_____

_____

_____

_____

_____

_____

_____

_____

# EDITING

Study the following exercises and complete them as quickly as possible. Think about them in connection with your paragraph. When you finish the exercises, edit your paragraph and give it to your teacher. If necessary, make changes in grammar, punctuation, and any other item.

## Exercise A. Pronouns

*Directions:* Put in **he, my,** or **his.**

_____ is Osman Hersey. _____ is about 58 years old. _____
       1                            2                                3
is about 1.7 meters tall, and _____ weight is about 65 kg.
                                     4
_____ is a vegetable farmer near Mogadiscio, Somalia. _____
      5                                                                6
farm has at least 100 hectares. In addition to me, _____ father
                                                           7
has six children, four daughters, and one son. _____ works
                                                      8
hard to give us a good life. _____ wants _____ children to
                                    9              10
work hard too. _____ always tells me to do _____ best.
                     11                              12

## Exercise B.  Punctuation and capitalization

*Directions:*  Names of people, cities, countries, and companies begin with capital letters. Punctuate the following paragraph and correct the capitalization.

my father is mohammed al-tamimi   he is about 50 years old   he is tall and thin   i don't know exactly how tall he is   and i don't know how much he weighs   he has black hair   a moustache   and a goatee   he is a car dealer in riyadh   saudi arabia   he sells mercedes benz and porsche cars   his company is large   more than 50 people work for him   my father is very smart   i love my father   but i don't see him a lot   usually he is at his company or with my brothers   i think that he is the best father in the world to his fifteen children

## Exercise C.  Sentence order

*Directions:*  Place the words in the right order. Be sure to capitalize and punctuate correctly. Some items may have more than one possible order.

**1.** least, 100, farm, at, has, his, hectares

_____

**2.** about, old, is, years, 58, he

_____

**3.** best, my, do, to, he, me, tells, always

_____

**4.** farmer, a, vegetable, is, he, near, Mogadiscio

_____

5. he, life, works, good, a, us, give, to, hard

_____

6. wants, children, he, his, to, too, work, hard

_____

7. six, children, my, father, has

_____

# PARAGRAPH
## 3

*Write about your classmate.*

## PREWRITING

Read and discuss the following paragraph about Ursula Kaaris with your class. How does the writer describe Ursula's face (in what order)? Are there any parts of her face not described?

My classmate is Ursula Kaaris. She is 18 years old, and she is from Hillerod, Denmark. Her face is oblong. Her hair is short and blonde. Her ears are small. Her eyebrows are thin, and her eyelashes are long. Her eyes are blue. Her nose is not short and not long. Her cheeks are white and smooth. Her mouth is small, and her lips are thin and red. She is wearing an unusual purple-colored lipstick that matches her purple fingernails. In Denmark, Ursula is a university student. She doesn't know what job she wants in the future. She wants to travel a lot in the United States.

The following cluster was made by the writer.

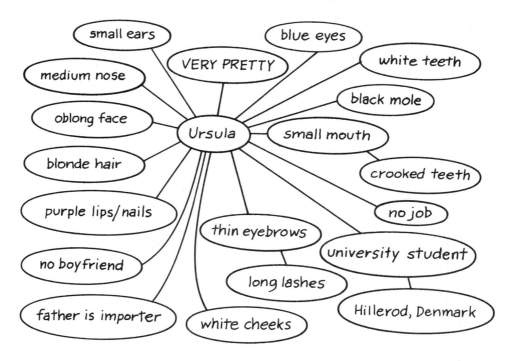

Again, notice what information the writer uses, and does not use. What are five items the writer does not use? Why not?

Your teacher will now pair you with another student in the class. Make a cluster of your ideas about your classmate. First, introduce yourself; next, ask some questions, such as name, native country, field of study, goal in life; finally, describe the person physically.

# WRITING

Use the cluster to write a paragraph about your classmate. Again, you don't have to use all of the cluster, and you may add information not in the cluster. Don't worry about grammar here.

_____

_____

_____

_____

_____

_____

_____

_____

_____

_____

_____

_____

_____

_____

_____

_____

_____

## SHARING

Ask your classmate (the person you described) to read your paragraph and tell you what he or she likes or doesn't like. What do you think should be changed?

## REVISING

Rewrite your paragraph. Change whatever you want. Try to give a clear picture of your classmate.

_____

_____

_____

_____

_____

_____

_____

_____

_____

_____

_____

_____

_____

_____

_____

_____

# EDITING

Study the following exercises. When you finish, edit your paragraph and give it to your teacher.

### Exercise A. Verbs and pronouns

_Directions:_ Put in **is, are, he, his,** or **my.**

_____ classmate is Ernesto Lopez. He _____ 22 years old.
    1                                                          2

_____ is from Buenos Aires, Argentina. Ernesto _____ a
    3                                                                      4

winemaker in Buenos Aires. _____ wants to study enology at
                                              5

an American university. _____ face _____ round. His hair
                                          6                7

_____ medium length and blonde. _____ ears _____ small.
    8                                                    9              10

His eyebrows _____ thick. _____ eyes are green. His nose
                      11                    12

_____ long. _____ cheeks _____ red and rough. _____ mouth
    13              14                  15                                16

_____ small. Ernesto _____ a very friendly person.
    17                            18

## Exercise B. Compound sentences

**Directions:** A **comma** and a **coordinate conjunction** can join two sentences. In each of the following items, form a single compound sentence out of the two sentences given.

**Example:** She is 18 years old. She is from Hillerod, Denmark. She is 18 years old, and she is from Hillerod, Denmark.

1. Her face is oblong. Her hair is short.

   _____

2. Ernesto is a winemaker. He wants to study enology at an American university.

   _____

3. Her eyelashes are long. Her eyes are blue.

   _____

4. She is 18 years old. She is from Hillerod, Denmark.

   _____

5. His eyebrows are thick. His eyes are green.

   _____

## Exercise C. Adjectives and nouns

**Directions:** Fill in the blanks with any adjective or noun. Use your imagination.

One of my friends in this class is Anabel Tatis. She is a

young _____. She is from _____. Her face is
            1                                    2

_____. Her hair is _____ and _____.
            3                              4                    5

Her ears are _____. Her eyebrows are _____
                      6                                        7

and _____. Her mouth is _____. Today
          8                              9

Anabel is wearing a _____ skirt and a _____
                          10                          11

blouse. Her _____ are _____ . Anabel
                  12                  13

is a _____ in her country. She wants to study
          14

_____ in the United States. After her studies,
      15

she wants to travel to _____ , _____ ,
                            16                  17

and _____ . In her free time, Anabel likes to play
          18

_____ and _____ . She is a very
      19                  20

_____ person.
      21

# PARAGRAPH
## 4

*Write about the place where you live.*

# PREWRITING

Read the following paragraph silently. Write down three reasons why you would not like to live in the apartment. Think about the specific information in the paragraph. Discuss your ideas with the class.

My American roommate and I have a simple apartment at 237 Cranbrook Court. It is a medium-sized apartment. It has a kitchen, living room, bedroom, and bathroom. In the kitchen, there are an old wooden table, four new metal and plastic chairs, an electric stove, a small General Electric refrigerator, and lots of dirty dishes in the sink. Sometimes, at night, we have mice and bugs on the kitchen floor. The living room has a brown vinyl sofa with lots of holes in it, one table with a broken lamp, and one big green chair. Pictures of Madonna and Maradona are on the wall. The bedroom has two desks, two lamps, a small chest of drawers, two beds, and piles of dirty clothes. The bathroom has a toilet, bathtub, sink, and mirror. The shower doesn't work. Our apartment is OK, but it is not fantastic.

Reason 1 _____

Reason 2 _____

Reason 3 _____

The paragraph has many specific details such as: *237 Cranbrook Court*; a small *General Electric* refrigerator; a *brown vinyl* sofa; pictures of *Madonna* and *Maradona*. Try to make the following details more specific:

**1.** in the _____ kitchen

**2.** a _____ electric stove

**3.** one _____ table

**4.** on the _____ wall

**5.** two _____ beds

**6.** the _____ bathroom

Think about the place where you live. Try to remember as many details as possible. Make a cluster.

## WRITING

Now give your cluster to one of your classmates. Write a paragraph using *another person's* cluster. Feel free to make changes as you write.

_____

_____

_____

_____

_____

_____

_____

_____

_____

_____

_____

_____

_____

_____

## SHARING

Give your paragraph to the person whose cluster you were using. Now look at the paragraph that is about the place where you live. Is it a good description? Is the information communicated clearly?

## REVISING

Rewrite your classmate's paragraph about the place where you live. You may change words, phrases, sentences, or the whole paragraph.

_____

_____

_____

_____

_____

_____

_____

_____

_____

_____

_____

_____

## EDITING

Complete the following exercises. Then edit your paragraph and submit it to your teacher.

**Exercise A.** Verbs

*Directions:*  Put in **is, are, have,** or **has.**

My Chinese friend and I _____ an apartment on Russell St.
                          1
It _____ a very small apartment. It _____ a kitchen/living
   2                                3
room, bedroom, and bathroom. The kitchen _____ a plastic
                                          4
table, two chairs, a gas stove, and a small refrigerator. We

_____ an old Zenith TV and some cushions in the living room.
5

There _____ four pictures on the wall: a white kitten, yellow
       6
flowers, a girl with a violin, and a reprint of Van Gogh. The

bedroom _____ two beds, two desks, and two lamps. There
         7

_____ one dresser for our clothes. The bathroom _____ a
8                                                  9
toilet, shower, sink, and mirror. Our apartment _____ always
                                                 10
clean because my roommate is crazy about cleaning.

**Exercise B.**  Punctuation and capitalization

*Directions:*  Put in periods, capitals, and commas. Names of
               apartment buildings and streets start with a capital

letter. Items in series have a comma between them.

***Example:***   It has a kitchen, living room, and bedroom.

my american roommate and i have a simple apartment at 237 cranbrook court it is a medium-sized apartment it has a kitchen living room bedroom and bathroom in the kitchen there are an old wooden table four new metal and plastic chairs an electric stove a small general electric refrigerator and lots of dirty dishes in the sink sometimes at night we have mice and bugs on the kitchen floor the living room has a brown vinyl sofa with lots of holes in it one table with a broken lamp and one big green chair pictures of madonna and maradona are on the wall the bedroom has two desks two lamps a small chest of drawers two beds and piles of dirty clothes the bathroom has a toilet bathtub sink and mirror the shower doesn't work our apartment is OK but it is not fantastic

## Exercise C. Sentence order

***Directions:***   Place the words in the right order. Be sure to put a capital letter at the beginning of each sentence and a period at the end of the sentence.

1. Chinese, I, apartment, live, my, and, friend, in, an

   _____

2. small, is, apartment, it, a

   _____

3. we, an, old, have, TV

   _____

**4.** four, the, wall, on, pictures, are, there

_____

**5.** two, bedroom, has, the, beds

_____

**6.** apartment, clean, always, is, our

_____

# PARAGRAPH
# 5

*Write about your home city and its people.*

# PREWRITING

Read the following paragraphs about Rome. Then discuss both paragraphs with your class. Which one gives you the most information about Rome? Fill in the outline with your class.

I am from Rome. Rome is in Italy, and it is the magnificent capital of Italy. It is a very large city. It has many people. Rome usually has nice weather because it is close to the sea. Rome also has many famous fantastic things to see. Rome also has many beautiful parks. Romans like to walk in the parks, and we like to sit in the comfortable cafes. We like to watch people, and we are always in love. Every Roman likes to have fun, and Rome is a great city to have fun in!

I am from Rome. Rome is in southern Italy, and it is the magnificent capital of Italy. It is a very large city. It has about three million people. Rome usually has warm weather because it is close to the Mediterranean Sea. Rome also has many fantastic things to see. For example, the Vatican, the Colosseum, and the Trevi Fountains are in Rome. Rome also has many beautiful parks. Romans like to walk in the parks, and we like to sit in the comfortable cafes. We like to watch people, and we are always in love. Every Roman likes to have fun, and Rome is a great city to have fun in!

### Outline

City  _____

**I.** Geographical location  _____

**II.** Population  _____

**III.** Climate  _____

**IV.** Things to see  _____

_____

_____

**V.** What Romans do    _____

_____

_____

Make a cluster about your native city. Include some of its good points and bad points.

> native city:
> _____

# WRITING

Write a paragraph using your cluster. Be relaxed, and concentrate on your ideas.

_____

_____

_____

_____

_____

_____

_____

_____

_____

_____

_____

_____

_____

_____

## SHARING

Ask one of your classmates to read your paragraph to you. What do you think? Can you understand everything you have written? Does the reader understand your ideas?

## REVISING

Revise your paragraph. Continue to concentrate on ideas. Think about the order of your ideas. Put the most important point last.

_____

_____

_____

_____

_____

_____

_____

_____

_____

_____

_____

_____

_____

_____

_____

_____

# EDITING

Think about your paragraph as you do the following exercises. When you finish, edit your paragraph and give it to your teacher.

## Exercise A. Verbs

*Directions:*  Put in **am, is, are, has, have,** or **like.**

I _____ from Shagra. Shagra _____ in central Jordan.
       1                              2

Shagra _____ a medium-sized city; it _____ about 30,000
         3                                4

people. The weather _____ very hot in Shagra because it
                       5

_____ in the desert. The temperature _____ usually 42–46°C
  6                                        7

in the summer. Nothing famous _____ in Shagra. My town
                                 8

_____ many markets, shops, and stores, but no large build-
  9

ings _____ in Shagra. The people of Shagra _____ to sit in
       10                                      11

the cafes, go to the mosques, and visit their friends' houses.

Shagra _____ a normal city, and I _____ many friends
         12                            13

there.

## Exercise B. Compound sentences

*Directions:*   Join the sentences.

1.  Romans like to walk in the parks. **(and)** We like to sit in the cafes.

    _____

2.  We like to watch people. **(and)** We are always in love.

    _____

3.  My town has many markets. **(but)** No large buildings are there.

    _____

4.  It is a very large city. **(and)** It has about three million lovely people.

    _____

## Exercise C. Articles

*Directions:*   Put in **a, an, the,** or leave the space blank.

1.  I am from _____ Rome.
2.  Rome is in _____ southern Italy, and it is _____ capital of Italy.
3.  It is _____ very large city.
4.  It has about _____ three million people.
5.  _____ Rome usually has warm weather because it is close to _____ Mediterranean Sea.
6.  _____ Rome also has many famous things to see.
7.  For example, _____ Vatican, _____ Colosseum, and _____ Trevi Fountains are in _____ Rome.
8.  Romans like to walk in _____ parks, and we like to sit in _____ cafes.
9.  _____ Rome is _____ great city to have fun in.

# PARAGRAPH
## 6

*Write about what your classmate's mother does every day.*

## PREWRITING

Read the following paragraph silently. When you finish, do the exercise with one of your classmates.

Rachel's mother, Ruth, has a busy and interesting life. Ruth usually wakes up at 6:30 A.M. Then she likes to lie in bed for a while and drink coffee. After about half an hour, she likes to get up and go to work on the trees and flowers around the apartment. At about 8:00 she goes back inside and takes a shower. Then she dresses, and she goes to exercise with her friends. When she finishes her exercises, she goes shopping. She comes home at around 10:30, cleans the house, and cooks some lunch. From 12:00 to 12:30, she eats lunch with her husband, Shuka. From then until 7:30, she teaches piano, organ, and accordion to her students. When she finishes, she eats dinner with her husband. In the evening she likes to play cards or go dancing. At about 11:30, she and her husband usually go to sleep.

Look at the following schedule. What are five instances in which the schedule is not the same as in the paragraph?

| | |
|---|---|
| 6:30 A.M. | wakes up |
| 6:30–7:00 | lies in bed/drinks coffee |
| 7:00 | gets dressed, works on flowers |
| 8:00–10:30 | takes a shower |
| | finishes exercises, goes shopping |
| 11:00–12:00 | comes home/cleans/cooks |
| 12:00–12:30 P.M. | eats lunch with her husband |
| 1:00–7:30 | teaches piano, organ, and accordion |
| 7:30 | goes dancing |
| 11:00 | goes to sleep |

Now, ask your classmate about her or his mother. Write down, in schedule form, at least eight things your classmate's mother does every day.

### *Schedule*

_____

_____

_____

_____

_____

_____

_____

_____

_____

_____

_____

_____

_____

_____

# WRITING

Use the schedule to write a paragraph about your class-mate's mother.

_____

_____

_____

_____

_____

_____

_____

_____

_____

_____

_____

_____

_____

## SHARING

Show your paragraph to your classmate. Ask your classmate to make at least *three* changes in the paragraph (add, reorder, subtract).

## REVISING

Revise the paragraph using changes your classmate suggested.

_____

_____

_____

_____

_____

_____

_____

_____

_____

_____

_____

_____

_____

_____

_____

_____

_____

_____

# EDITING

Think about your paragraph as you do these exercises. Then edit your paragraph and submit it.

**Exercise A.** Verbs

**_Directions:_**  Choose the right verb. Make it **third person singular.**

| | | | |
|---|---|---|---|
| go (2) | clean | read | leave |
| make (2) | eat | watch | get |
| come | take | sew | |

Her mother, Hisae, _____ up at 6:00 A.M. every day.
<br>1

From 6:00 to 7:00 A.M., she _____ breakfast for the family.
<br>2

At 7:00 A.M. she _____ the house and _____ shopping.
<br>3 4

She _____ back at 10:00 A.M. and _____ the house.
<br>5 6

She _____ lunch by herself at 12:30 P.M. In the afternoon,
<br>7

she usually _____ a nap from 2:00 to 4:00 P.M. From 4:00
<br>8

to 6:00 P.M., she _____ her favorite TV programs. At 6:00
<br>9

P.M. she _____ dinner for the family. After dinner, she
<br>10

_____ novels and _____ . She _____ to sleep with
<br>11 12 13

her husband at about 10:30 P.M.

## Exercise B. Punctuation and capitalization

***Directions:***   Put in capital letters, periods, and commas.

rachel's mother ruth has a busy and interesting life ruth usually wakes up at 6:30 A.M. then she likes to lie in bed for a while and drink coffee after about half an hour she likes to get up and go to work on the trees and flowers around the apartment at about 8:00 she goes back inside and takes a shower then she dresses and she goes to exercise with her friends when she finishes her exercises she goes shopping she comes home at around 10:30 cleans the house and cooks some lunch from 12:00 to 12:30 she eats lunch with her husband shuka from then until 7:30 she teaches piano organ and accordion to her students when she finishes she eats dinner with her husband in the evening she likes to play cards or go dancing at about 11:30 she and her husband usually go to sleep

## Exercise C. Prepositions of time

***Directions:***   Put in **at, from . . . to,** or **in.**

1. She usually wakes up _____ 6:30 A.M.
2. _____ 6:30 _____ 7:00 she lies in bed and drinks coffee.
3. _____ 7:00 she likes to get up and go to work on the flowers around the house.
4. She comes home _____ 10:30, cleans the house, and cooks some lunch.
5. _____ 12:00 _____ 12:30, she eats lunch with her husband.
6. _____ the evening she likes to play cards or go dancing.
7. _____ 11:30 she and her husband go to sleep.

## Exercise D.  Paragraph order

> *Directions:*  These sentences are not in the right order. Copy
> them in the right order in paragraph form on a
> piece of paper.

She comes back at 10:00 A.M. and cleans the house. From
4:00 to 6:00 P.M., she watches her favorite TV programs. She
goes to sleep with her husband at about 10:30 P.M. She eats
lunch by herself at 12:30 P.M. Her mother, Hisae, gets up at
6:00 A.M. everyday. After dinner, she reads novels and sews.
In the afternoon, she usually takes a nap from 2:00 to 4:00 P.M.
From 6:00 to 7:00 A.M., she makes breakfast for the family. At
7:00 A.M. she leaves the house and goes shopping. At 6:00
P.M. she makes dinner for the family.

# PARAGRAPH
# 7

*Write about what you are doing right now.*

# PREWRITING

Read the following paragraph aloud with your class; then discuss the questions after the paragraph.

I am sitting on the wet grass outside our English classroom. There is a lot of trash on the ground. I am sitting under a big oak tree. The sun is not shining. Big, black clouds are moving across the sky. The wind is blowing hard. Some cups are blowing across the lawn. A crow is flying in the wind. I see many people. Some are walking to their classes. Some are going to the library. Only our class is sitting on the grass. Two guys are slowly riding by on their bicycles. I think they are talking and laughing, but I can't hear them. They are wearing heavy coats. I am wearing only a thin sweater. Because it is cold, I am stopping.

## *Questions*

1. What season of the year do you think it is?
2. What kind of trash do you think is on the ground?
3. What change in weather do you think is about to happen?
4. Why are the guys riding slowly?
5. Why can't the writer hear the guys?
6. Why do you think the grass is wet?
7. Why do you think the class is sitting outside on the wet grass?

If it isn't too cold or wet, go outside with your class and find a comfortable place to sit. Make a cluster of things you feel, hear, or see.

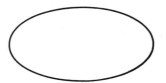

## WRITING

Use the cluster to write a paragraph. Write as if what you feel, hear, and see is *now*.

_____

_____

_____

_____

_____

_____

_____

_____

_____

_____

_____

_____

_____

## SHARING

Read your paragraph to a small group of your classmates. Ask them what they think. Do they understand everything? Did you communicate your feelings and observations well?

After you hear from your classmates, read your paragraph again. Is there anything you want to change?

## REVISING

Rewrite your paragraph. Change whatever you want.

_____

_____

_____

_____

_____

_____

_____

_____

_____

_____

_____

_____

# EDITING

Edit your paragraph after completing these exercises.

**Exercice A.  Verbs**

*Directions:*  Put in the right form of the **present continuous.**

I (sit) _____ in Shields Library on the UCD campus. I
                1
(sit) _____ at a large brown table with two students.
          2
They (study) _____ mathematics. They (talk)
                    3
_____ very quietly. Several students (look) _____
        4                                                    5
for books in the stacks. One student (drink) _____ water
                                                  6
from a water fountain. He (hit) _____ himself in the eye
                                      7
with the water. One boy at another table (scratch) _____
                                                          8
his head with his pencil. The air conditioner (blow) _____
                                                            9
cold air at me. I (move) _____ because I don't want to
                              10
get sick.

**Exercice B.  Sentence order**

*Directions:*  Place the words in the right order. Be sure to put a
                capital letter at the beginning of each sentence
                and a period at the end of each sentence.

1.  sitting, wet, I, am, grass, the, on

    _____

2.  a, tree, under, sitting, am, I, big, oak

    _____

**3.** sun, is, the, shining, not

_____

**4.** big, are, sky, across, clouds, moving, the

_____

**5.** is, blowing, wind, hard, the

_____

**6.** classes, to, walking, some, are, their, students

_____

**7.** to, students, going, library, some, are, the

_____

**8.** coats, are, they, wearing, heavy

_____

**9.** sweater, only, am, wearing, thin, I, a

_____


## Exercise C.  Prepositions of space and direction

_Directions:_  Put in **on, under, across, in,** or **to.**

**1.** I am sitting _____ the wet grass.

**2.** I am sitting _____ a big tree.

**3.** Big, black clouds are moving _____ the sky.

**4.** A bird is flying _____ the wind.

**5.** Some are walking _____ their classes.

**6.** Some are going _____ the library.

**7.** Our class is sitting _____ the grass.

**8.** Two guys are slowly riding by _____ their bicycles.

# PARAGRAPH
# 8

*Write about your favorite teacher (before now).*

## PREWRITING

Read and discuss the following paragraph about Mr. Aoki with your class. The paragraph was written by Shige Matsunori. What does Shige think about Mr. Aoki? What do you?

My favorite teacher was Mr. Kenji Aoki. He was a small, old man with gray hair and a gray beard. He was my fifth-grade mathematics teacher in Osaka, Japan. Mr. Aoki was hard, but friendly. For me, mathematics was a terrible subject. Many of my classmates were very good in math, but I was not. I had many problems, but Mr. Aoki was usually ready to help me, especially after class. His class was very difficult. We had a test every two days. Every night there were at least fifteen pages of homework. Many nights I was sick of math, but the homework was important. I was sorry at the end of the year. Mr. Aoki was a good teacher, and he helped me a lot.

Fill in the empty places in the cluster that Shige made.

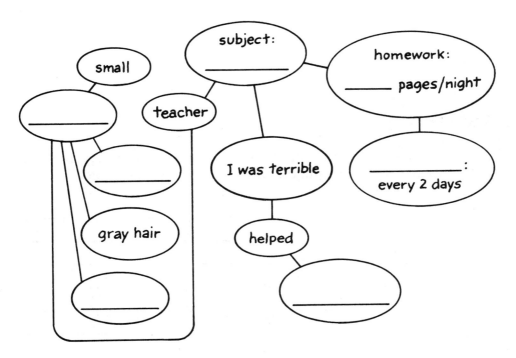

Make a cluster about your favorite teacher. Try to remember why you liked her or him. Try to remember specific examples.

## WRITING

Write a paragraph based on your cluster. Try hard to make your classmates understand why you remember the teacher so well.

_____

_____

_____

_____

_____

_____

_____

_____

_____

_____

_____

_____

_____

_____

## SHARING

Exchange your cluster from the Prewriting section for that of a classmate. On a separate piece of paper write a paragraph based on your classmate's cluster, while he or she writes a paragraph based on yours. When you finish, trade paragraphs with your classmate. Compare your classmate's paragraph with your paragraph in the Writing section. Both paragraphs are based on the same cluster. How are the paragraphs similar? How are they different?

## REVISING

Rewrite the paragraph you wrote in the Writing section. You may use some of your classmate's words or sentences if you want.

_____

_____

_____

_____

_____

_____

_____

_____

_____

_____

_____

_____

_____

_____

# EDITING

Before you edit your paragraph, complete the following exercises.

**Exercise A.** Verbs

*Directions:* Put in **was** or **were**.

My best teacher _____ Ms. Sylvie Goncourt. She _____ a
                   1                                    2
young woman with brown hair and glasses. She _____ my
                                             3
eighth-grade French teacher in Antwerp, Belgium. Ms.
Goncourt's explanations _____ clear and interesting. She
                        4
_____ close to her students. French _____ an easy subject
5                                      6
for me in general, but some things _____ difficult, such as
                                   7
grammar and composition. Ms. Goncourt _____ able to ex-
                                      8
plain the most difficult points very easily and clearly. Also, most
of her classes _____ very interesting because there _____
               9                                       10
something new every day. I _____ lucky to have Ms. Sylvie
                          11
Goncourt as my teacher.

## Exercise B. Punctuation and capitalization

> *Directions:* Put in periods, capitals, and commas. Names of cities and countries should be separated by commas.

my favorite teacher was mr kenji aoki he was a small old man with gray hair and a gray beard he was my fifth-grade mathematics teacher in osaka japan mr aoki was hard but friendly for me mathematics was a terrible subject many of my classmates were very good in math but i was not i had many problems but mr aoki was usually ready to help me especially after class his class was very difficult we had a test every two days every night there were at least fifteen pages of homework many nights i was sick of math but the homework was important i was sorry at the end of the year mr aoki was a good teacher and he helped me a lot

## Exercise C. Compound sentences

> *Directions:* Join the sentences with a comma and conjunction.

1. Many of my classmates were very good in math. **(but)** I was not.

   _____

2. I had many problems. **(but)** Mr. Aoki was always ready to help me.

   _____

3. Many nights I was sick of math. **(but)** The homework was important.

   _____

**4.** Ms. Goncourt's explanations were clear and interesting. **(and)** She was close to her students.

---

## Exercise D.  Pronouns

*Directions:*  Change the terms in dark type to **she, he, her,** or **his.**

1. **Ms. Sylvie Goncourt** ( *she* ) was a young woman with brown hair and glasses.
2. **Ms. Goncourt** (        ) was my eighth-grade French teacher.
3. I had many problems, but **Mr. Aoki** (        ) was always ready to help me.
4. **Mr. Aoki's** (        ) class was very difficult.
5. Most of **Ms. Goncourt's** (        ) classes were very interesting.
6. I was lucky to have **Ms. Sylvie Goncourt** (        ) as my teacher.
7. **Mr. Aoki** (        ) was a good teacher, and he helped me a lot.

# PARAGRAPH
# 9

*Write about an old car, motorcycle, bicycle, or some other means of transportation you had.*

## PREWRITING

Read the following paragraph silently, and then fill in the diagram after the paragraph.

My uncle Lars's old car was a 1968 144S Volvo. When it was new, it was pretty. It was yellow on the outside, but it had black seats. It was a standard-sized sedan, with four doors. The seats were large and comfortable, and the car had enough room for five people. On the right side of the dashboard, there was an AM radio. The Volvo had an automatic transmission and a diesel engine. I remember the car clearly because it was the first car I drove. By that time it was old, and it always broke down.

Now fill in this organizational diagram.

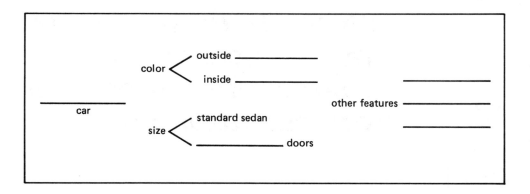

Make a cluster about an old car or some means of transportation that you, your parents, or a friend had. Include specific facts such as year, model, and so on. If you can't remember exactly, invent.

## WRITING

Use your cluster to write a paragraph. Don't worry about grammar. Feel free to make changes as you write.

_____

_____

_____

_____

_____

_____

_____

_____

_____

_____

_____

_____

_____

_____

## SHARING

Give your paragraph to three people in your class, and ask each one of them to write two changes. After you get your paragraph back, look at their suggestions.

Do you think their changes help or hurt your paragraph? Ask them why they think the changes are good.

## REVISING

Rewrite your paragraph. Concentrate on ideas, but also think about vocabulary and organization.

_____

_____

_____

_____

_____

_____

_____

_____

_____

_____

_____

_____

_____

_____

# EDITING

Use these exercises to help you in editing your own paragraph.

## Exercise A.  Verbs

_Directions:_  Put in **was, were,** or **had.**

My first car _____ a 1968 Plymouth GTX. It _____ a
<sub>1</sub> ... <sub>2</sub>
cheap, used car, but I _____ proud of it. The car _____ blue
<sub>3</sub> ... <sub>4</sub>
on the outside and blue on the inside. It _____ medium-sized
<sub>5</sub>
with two front seats, a back seat, and two doors. The front

seats _____ small, and the back seat _____ only big enough
<sub>6</sub> ... <sub>7</sub>
for two people. On the dashboard, it _____ a stereo tape
<sub>8</sub>
player and an AM-FM radio. My GTX _____ a manual four-
<sub>9</sub>
speed transmission, and it _____ a big engine (440 cu. in.). I
<sub>10</sub>
_____ a lot of problems with the car, but I also _____ a lot
<sub>11</sub> ... <sub>12</sub>
of fun in it.

## Exercise B.  Punctuation and capitalization

_Directions:_  Put in capitals, periods, and commas.

my uncle lars's old car was a 1968 144S volvo when it was
new it was pretty it was yellow on the outside but it had black

seats it was a standard-sized sedan with four doors the seats were large and comfortable and the car had enough room for five people on the right side of the dashboard there was an AM radio the volvo had an automatic transmission and a diesel engine i remember the car clearly because it was the first car i drove by that time it was old and it always broke down

## Exercise C.  Compound sentences

***Directions:***   Look at the Volvo paragraph and the paragraph in Exercise A. Copy the seven compound sentences you see.

Volvo Paragraph:

1. _____
   _____

2. _____
   _____

3. _____
   _____

Paragraph in Exercise A:

4. _____
   _____

5. _____
   _____

6. _____
   _____

7. _____
   _____

# PARAGRAPH
## 10

*Write about what you did last weekend, or on a recent trip.*

## PREWRITING

Read and discuss the following paragraph with your class. Complete the organizational diagram by yourself, then compare your answers with those of your classmates.

Last Sunday, my friends and I went to San Francisco. We visited Golden Gate Park, Chinatown, and Fisherman's Wharf. At 10:00 in the morning we went to the Steinhart Aquarium in the Park. We saw many different kinds of sharks, fish, and crazy people. After two hours, we drove to Chinatown. We ate lunch there. We had almond chicken, mushi pork, and steamed rice. I got a fortune cookie that said "you will inherit a million dollars." At about 2:00 we took an exciting ride in a cable car to Fisherman's Wharf. While we were there, we took a boat ride around the bay, we shopped at Pier 39 and the Cannery, and we all drank milkshakes at an ice cream store at Ghirardelli Square. When we went back to our car at 5:00, we found a $25.00 ticket on the windshield.

| | Golden Gate Park | _____ | _____ |
|---|---|---|---|
| | | | _____ |
| | | | crazy people |
| | _____ | lunch | _____ |
| | | | _____ |
| city | | | _____ |
| | | | fortune cookie |
| | _____ | | |
| | | Pier 39 | |
| | | _____ | |
| | | Ghirardelli Square | |

Think about what you did last weekend, or remember a trip you took to some place. Make a cluster of all of your experiences.

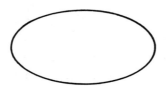

# WRITING

Write a paragraph based on your cluster. Try to include as many examples as possible.

_____

_____

_____

_____

_____

_____

_____

_____

_____

_____

_____

_____

_____

_____

## SHARING

Give your paragraph to a classmate. Ask your classmate to draw a diagram of your paragraph (similar to the one on page 62) while you draw a diagram of your classmate's paragraph.

## REVISING

Look at the diagram that your classmate drew. Did your classmate understand your ideas and organization? Rewrite your paragraph, making any changes you think are necessary.

_____

_____

_____

_____

_____

_____

_____

_____

_____

_____

_____

_____

_____

# EDITING

Think about your paragraph as you complete these exercises. Then edit your paragraph.

**Exercise A.** Subordinate clauses

*Directions:* Your teacher will explain what a complex sentence is. Change each of these to a complex sentence.

*Example:* **(After)** We visited Underground Atlanta. We went to a baseball game.

After we visited Underground Atlanta, we went to a baseball game.

1. **(While)** We were in Atlanta. We visited Underground Atlanta, Peachtree Street, and Stone Mountain.

_____

2. **(After)** We stayed in Underground Atlanta for two hours. We shopped on Peachtree Street.

_____

3. We finished shopping. **(Before)** We went to Stone Mountain.

_____

4. We took a bus. **(When)** We went to Stone Mountain.

_____

5. **(While)** We were at Stone Mountain. We rode a train.

_____

## Exercise B. Prepositions

*Directions:* Put in **at, around, to, of,** or **in.**

Last Sunday, my friends and I went _____ San Francisco. _____ 10:00 in the morning we went _____ the
Steinhart Aquarium _____ the park. We saw many different
kinds _____ sharks and fish. After two hours, we drove
_____ Chinatown. _____ about 2:00 we took a cable
car _____ Fisherman's Wharf. We took a boat ride
_____ the bay, and we shopped _____ Pier 39 and the
Cannery. We all drank milkshakes _____ an ice-cream
store _____ Ghirardelli Square.

## Exercise C. Sentence order

*Directions:* Put the words in correct order.

1. Francisco, to, my, and, I, friends, went, San

   _____

2. different, many, kinds, saw, we, of, sharks

   _____

3. drove, we, Chinatown, to

   _____

4. Fisherman's Wharf, car, to, cable, took, we, the

   _____

5. we, bay, around, ride, boat, the, took, a

   _____

**6.** all, we, drank, milkshakes

_____

**7.** came, at, 5:00, we, home   (2 ways)

_____

_____

# PARAGRAPH
# 11

*Write about your classmate's best childhood friend.*

# PREWRITING

Read and discuss the following paragraph with your class. Make a list of ten things you do not know about Masoume Abbas. Would the paragraph be better with some of these things included?

My classmate is Fatima Sharadi of Tehran, Iran. When she was a child, her best friend was Masoume Abbas. Fatima and Masoume went to kindergarten and elementary school together in Tehran. They also had the same piano teacher. They did many things together. They played games in the park, sang songs, and did their homework together. Sometimes their families went on vacation to the Caspian Sea together. One time they had a fight that lasted two years, but they became friends again. After elementary school, they went to different middle schools, high schools, and universities. Today they still write letters and make telephone calls to each other.

1. _____
2. _____
3. _____
4. _____
5. _____
6. _____
7. _____
8. _____
9. _____
10. _____

Interview one of your classmates. Ask these questions (and any others you think of) about her or his best childhood friend.

What was your friend's name?

How long have you known your friend?

How did you first meet your friend? How old were you?

Please describe your friend.

What were some of the things you did together?

What was the funniest time you ever had together?

Did you ever get in trouble?

Are you still friends today?

## WRITING

Use the answers to write a paragraph. Remember to focus on ideas.

_____

_____

_____

_____

_____

_____

_____

_____

_____

_____

_____

_____

_____

_____

_____

_____

## SHARING

Give your paragraph to the classmate you interviewed. Take the paragraph based on the interview with you. What do you think? How could the paragraph about your childhood friend be better?

## REVISING

Rewrite the paragraph about your own childhood friend. You can take sentences out, add sentences, or reorder sentences.

_____

_____

_____

_____

_____

_____

_____

_____

_____

_____

_____

_____

_____

_____

_____

_____

## EDITING

Edit the revised paragraph after completing the following exercises.

### Exercise A.  Pronouns

*Directions:*  Put in **my, his, their, he, it,** or **they.**

_____ classmate's name is Beat Sarlos of Zermatt, Swit-
_____1_____
zerland. When _____ was a child, _____ best friend
                  2                      3
was Wilhelm Rizzoli. _____ lived on the same mountain,
                           4
and _____ was about 400 meters high. _____ went to
        5                                        6
elementary, secondary, and high schools together. _____
                                                        7
parents were also friends, so _____ slept at each other's
                                   8
house very often. _____ favorite activity was skiing;
                       9
_____ did _____ every day during the winter and
    10             11
spring. To have fun _____ used to put sticky stuff on the
                         12
bottom of tourist's skis so the skis wouldn't slide. When
_____ got older, _____ dated girls together every week-
    13                    14
end. Today, _____ are still good friends; Wilhelm wants to
                15
get _____ law degree in the United States, and Beat wants
        16
to get _____ medical degree here too.
            17

### Exercise B.  Punctuation and verbs

*Directions:*  Punctuate correctly and put in the correct **past
tense** form of the verb.

my classmate is fatima sharadi of tehran iran when she (be)

_____ a child her best friend (be) _____ masoume
         1                                        2

abbas fatima and masoume (go) _____ to kindergarten
                                   3

and elementary school together in tehran they also (have)

_____ the same piano teacher they (do) _____ many
         4                                        5

things together they (play) _____ games in the park (sing)
                                6

_____ songs and (do) _____ their homework together
         7                      8

sometimes their families (go) _____ on vacation to the
                                  9

caspian sea together one time they (have) _____ a fight
                                              10

that (last) _____ two years but they (become) _____
              11                                      12

friends again after elementary school they (go) _____ to
                                                    13

different middle schools high schools and universities today

they still write letters and make telephone calls to each other


## Exercise C. Articles

*Directions:* Put in **a, an, the,** or leave the space blank.

1. My classmate is Fatima Sharadi of _____ Tehran, Iran.
2. When she was _____ child, her best friend was _____
   Masoume Abbas.
3. Fatima and Masoume went to kindergarten and elementary
   school together in _____ Tehran.
4. They also had _____ same piano teacher.
5. They did _____ many things together.
6. They played games in _____ park, sang songs, and did
   their homework together.

7.  Sometimes their families went on vacation to _____ Caspian Sea together.

8.  After elementary school, they went to _____ different middle schools, high schools, and universities.

9.  Today, they still write _____ letters and make _____ telephone calls to each other.

# PARAGRAPH
## 12

*Write about how you used to spend your summers, or about a special summer.*

## PREWRITING

Read the following paragraph aloud with your class. Do you think the description is complete? Did the writer tell you what he or she saw? heard? felt? tasted? How could the paragraph be better?

My brother and I used to go to my grandfather's house in the Pyrenees mountains during our summer vacation. He lived in a two-story house beside the Aragon River. He used to wake up every morning at 5:30. Then we got in his small boat, and we went fishing. Usually, we didn't catch many fish, but many mosquitoes caught us. Around 7:00 we stopped fishing, we went back to the house, and my grandmother made breakfast for us. After breakfast, we walked 6 km. around a nearby mountain. On our walk we saw many animals such as birds, deer, and rabbits. In the afternoon, my brother and I swam in the river, and my grandparents slept in the house. At night, we all sat beside the river, and my grandfather told funny and scary stories. At 10:00 we went to sleep.

Make a kind of cluster that you think the writer used.

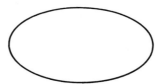

Now make a cluster about how you spent a special summer, or how you used to spend a typical summer. Use as many details as possible to make the reader feel what you felt.

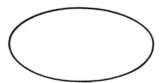

## WRITING

Use your cluster to write a paragraph. Feel free to make changes as you go. Remember that your teacher will not see this.

_____

_____

_____

_____

_____

_____

_____

_____

_____

_____

_____

_____

_____

_____

_____

_____

## SHARING

Read your paragraph very slowly to the entire class. Give everyone a chance to comment on your ideas. What problems do you see? What needs to be changed?

## REVISING

Using the comments of your classmates, rewrite your paragraph. Make sure your description is clear and complete.

_____

_____

_____

_____

_____

_____

_____

_____

_____

_____

_____

_____

_____

_____

# EDITING

After completing these exercises, edit your paragraph.

## Exercise A. Prepositions

*Directions:* Put in **beside, of, to, for, in,** or **at.**

When I was a child _____ Algeria, I used to spend most
1

_____ my summer vacations _____ the beach. My fam-
2                                   3

ily lived near Algiers, and my parents often took my sister and

me _____ a beach near Azeffoun. Azeffoun is _____
4                                                   5

the Mediterranean Sea; it had beautiful white beaches and

warm blue water. _____ course, we swam a lot _____
6                                   7

the beach, and we built a lot _____ sand castles. In addi-
8

tion, we spent many afternoons looking _____ sea shells,
9

and catching small fish. We also played a special kind

_____ racketball _____ the beach. Now, it is impossi-
10                      11

ble _____ swim near Azeffoun because the army has
12

made it a military base.

## Exercise B. Subordinate clauses

*Directions:* Make complex sentences.

1. **(After)** We got up in the morning. We went fishing.

   _____

2. We also played a special kind of racketball game. **(while)** We were at the beach.

   _____

3. My grandfather told funny and scary stories. **(while)** We sat beside the river.

   _____

4. **(When)** We walked around the mountain. We saw many animals.

   _____

## Exercise C. Paragraph order

*Directions:* Put the sentences in the right order, showing the correct time sequence.

After breakfast, we walked 6 km. around a nearby mountain. At 10:00 we went to sleep. Then we got in his small boat, and we went fishing. My brother and I used to go to my grandfather's house in the Pyrenees mountains during our summer vacation. In the afternoon, my brother and I swam in the river, and my grandparents slept in the house. Usually, we didn't catch many fish, but many mosquitoes caught us. At night, we all sat beside the river, and my grandfather told funny and scary stories. He lived in a two-story house beside the Aragon River. On our walk we saw many animals such as birds, deer, and rabbits. He used to wake up every morning at 5:30. Around 7:00 we stopped fishing, we went back to the house, and my grandmother made breakfast for us.

# PARAGRAPH
# 13

*Write about your most frightening experience.*

## PREWRITING

Have you ever been very afraid? What was the situation? How did it make you feel? Read and discuss the following paragraph about a terrifying plane ride.

My worst experience happened on an airplane about five years ago. It was in the summer. I was flying from Guadalajara to Mexico City. When the plane took off from Guadalajara, the wind was blowing, and it was raining hard. I was a little nervous. The plane was all right for about 30 minutes. I was listening to the music on the airplane's radio. Many people were talking. The stewardesses were serving drinks to the passengers. Suddenly, lightning struck one of the engines. The plane dropped rapidly. Some people were screaming, and the stewardesses were falling down. My heart was beating very fast. I thought I was going to die. But after about 30 seconds, the pilot started the engine. We landed safely. But I will never fly again when the weather is bad.

Notice how the writer makes you feel what happened. What do you see? hear? feel?

See    _____

       _____

       _____

       _____

Hear   _____

       _____

       _____

       _____

Feel   _____

       _____

_____

_____

Think about an experience that was terrifying to you.
Make a cluster of your thoughts, feelings, and observations.

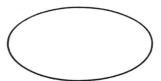

## WRITING

Change your cluster into a paragraph. Try to explain the
situation as clearly as possible. Try to make the reader feel
the situation.

_____

_____

_____

_____

_____

_____

_____

_____

_____

_____

_____

_____

_____

_____

_____

_____

## SHARING

Have another student read your paragraph aloud to you. Do you still feel the fear? Does your paragraph show the fear or excitement that you felt?

## REVISING

Are there any details that you have forgotten? Is there anything else you saw, heard, or felt? If so, add it to your paragraph now. Make any other changes you like.

_____

_____

_____

_____

_____

_____

_____
_____
_____
_____
_____
_____
_____
_____
_____
_____
_____

# EDITING

Use these exercises to help you edit your paragraph.

## Exercise A.  Verbs

*Directions:*  Put in the right form of the **past continuous** or **past tense.**

My worst experience (happen) _____ in a car on the

night I (graduate) _____ from my high school in Bang-
$\quad\quad\quad\quad\quad\quad\quad\quad\quad_2$

kok, Thailand. I (ride) _____ in my friend Tomo's car to a
$\quad\quad\quad\quad\quad\quad_3$

party when an accident (happen) _____. We (go)
$\quad\quad\quad\quad\quad\quad\quad\quad\quad\quad_4$

_____ to pick up our girlfriends when Tomo (lose)
$\quad_5$

_____ control of the car on a curve. The car (turn)
$\quad_6$

_____ upside down; as I (look) _____ out
$\quad_7$$\quad\quad\quad\quad\quad\quad\quad\quad\quad_8$

the window, everything (spin) _____ around. We
$\quad\quad\quad\quad\quad\quad\quad\quad_9$

(get) _____ out of the car fast, but as Tomo (get)
$\quad\quad_{10}$

_____ out of the car, he (cut) _____ his leg on
  11                                              12

some glass. Because Tomo (bleed) _____ badly, he
                                      13

was taken to a hospital. Fortunately, I (be) _____ not
                                                14

hurt, but I never (ride) _____ with Tomo again!
                            15


## Exercise B.  Punctuation, capitalization, and articles

*Directions:*   In the blank spaces add **a, an, the,** or leave the
                space empty. Fix the punctuation and capitaliza-
                tion.

my worst experience happened on _____ airplane about
                                    1

five years ago it was in _____ summer i was flying from
                            2

guadalajara to mexico city when _____ plane took off from
                                    3

guadalajara _____ wind was blowing and it was raining hard i
              4

was _____ little nervous _____ plane was all right for about 30
      5                     6

minutes i was listening to _____ music on _____ airplane's
                              7              8

radio many people were talking _____ stewardesses were serv-
                                   9

ing drinks to _____ passengers suddenly lightning struck one
                 10

of _____ engines _____ plane dropped rapidly _____ people
    11            12                            13

were screaming and _____ stewardesses were falling down
                       14

my heart was beating very fast i thought i was going to die but

after about 30 seconds _____ pilot started _____ engine we
                          15                  16

landed safely but i will never fly again when _____ weather is
                                                  17

bad

**Exercise C.** Complex sentences

> ***Directions:*** Look at Exercise A. Copy all of the complex sen-
> tences you see.

**1.** _____

_____

**2.** _____

_____

**3.** _____

_____

**4.** _____

_____

**5.** _____

_____

**6.** _____

_____

**Exercise D.** Adding specific details

> ***Directions:*** Add details to make these sentences in the air-
> plane paragraph more specific.

> ***Example:*** My worst experience happened on an airplane about
> five years ago. (What airplane?) (When, exactly?)
> My worst experience happened on <u>a Mexicana DC-7
> in August, 1980.</u>

**1.** When the plane took off from Guadalajara, the wind was
blowing. (What time of takeoff?) (How fast a wind?)

_____

**2.** I was listening to the music on the airplane's radio. (What kind of music?)

_____

**3.** Suddenly, lightning struck one of the engines. (Which side of the plane?)

_____

**4.** My heart was beating very fast. (About what heart rate?)

_____

# PARAGRAPH
# 14

*Write about what you are going to do this weekend.*

# PREWRITING

Where are you planning to go this weekend? What will you do when you get there? Read the paragraph silently and answer the questions. Then discuss the paragraph and answers with your class.

This week I am going to go to New York City. On Saturday morning, I am going to see the Statue of Liberty. Next, I am going to visit the United Nations. I want to talk with one of my friends from Burma, who is in the Burmese delegation. In the afternoon, I am going to shop on Fifth Avenue. I will buy some shoes for my father, a bag for my mother, and a wallet for my younger brother. In the evening, I really want to go to a baseball game in Yankee Stadium, between the Yankees and the Baltimore Orioles. On Sunday, I am going to spend the morning in Central Park, and the afternoon in the Metropolitan Museum of Art. Before I leave, I will send postcards to all of my friends in Rangoon. At about 5:00 P.M., I am going to return to Hartford.

### Questions

1. How long is the writer going to stay in New York?
2. Is the writer definitely from Burma?
3. Is the writer definitely going to the baseball game?
4. What are this person's main interests in going to New York?
5. What are the Yankees and Orioles?
6. What is Hartford?
7. Based on the information in the paragraph, what kind of personality do you think the writer has?

Think about the coming weekend. Where are you going to go? What are you going to do? (Even if you are not sure, imagine that you are.) Make a cluster about your coming activity.

## WRITING

Exchange clusters with one of your classmates. Write a
paragraph based on your classmate's cluster.

_____

_____

_____

_____

_____

_____

_____

_____

_____

_____

_____

_____

_____

_____

_____

_____

## SHARING

Give your paragraph to the person whose cluster you used. Take his or her paragraph and read it carefully. What problems do you see? Is the communication clear?

## REVISING

Rewrite your classmate's paragraph. Make any changes that you feel are appropriate. Try to improve the communication.

_____

_____

_____

_____

_____

_____

_____

_____

_____

_____

_____

_____

_____

_____

_____

# EDITING

After completing these exercises, submit your edited paragraph to your teacher.

### Exercise A. Prepositions

**_Directions:_**  Put in **of, on, in, at, up, to,** or **for.**

Unfortunately, I do not have enough money to travel, so this weekend I am going to stay _____ home. There are many things to do _____ my apartment _____ Saturday. I am going to take my dirty clothes _____ the laundry. After that, I will pick _____ the junk _____ my apartment. _____ the afternoon, I'm going to watch some sports _____ TV. _____ the evening, I will invite a few Sudanese friends _____ my apartment _____ a dinner _____ Sudanese shishkebobs. _____ Sunday I am going to study _____ my grammar test and go _____ the swimming pool. I think that will take care _____ my weekend.

### Exercise B. Subordinate clauses

**_Directions:_**  In these complex sentences, put **present tense** in the subordinate clause, and **future tense (will** or **going to)** in the independent clause.

*Example:*   **(After)** I will see the Statue of Liberty. I will visit the U.N.

After I see the Statue of Liberty, I will visit the U.N.
<u>subordinate clause</u>        <u>independent clause</u>

1. **(When)** I am going to shop on Fifth Avenue. I am going to buy some shoes for my father.

   _____

2. **(After)** I will send some postcards. I will return to Hartford.

   _____

3. I will go to the swimming pool. **(after)** I am going to study for my grammar test.

   _____

4. **(Before)** I will pick up the junk in my apartment. I am going to take my dirty clothes to the laundry.

   _____

## Exercise C.  Sentence order

*Directions:*   Put the words in the right order.

1. to, am, visit, going, Nations, the, United, I

   _____

2. of, one, friends, talk, going, Burma, from, my, I, am, to, with

   _____

3. I, baseball, game, going, Yankee, in, to, Stadium, am, go, a, to

   _____

4. pick, junk, up, my, I, will, the, in, apartment

   _____

5. going, Hartford, return, to, am, I, to

   _____

**6.** invite, will, I, Sudanese, friends, few, a, apartment, to, my

_____

**7.** weekend, my, of, care, take, will, that, think, I

_____

# PARAGRAPH
# 15

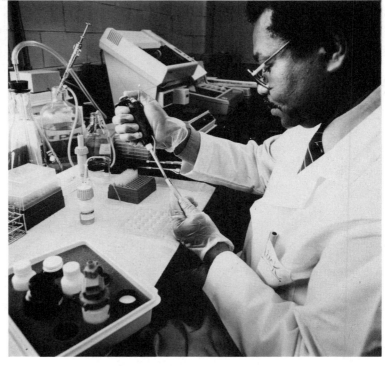

*Describe how the world will be in 2100.*

## PREWRITING

What will the future be like? No one knows, but everyone has an opinion. Read the following paragraph and complete the diagram. Discuss the paragraph and diagram with your class.

What will the world be like in the future? I think that future people will go through the same cycle of life and have the same problems as people today. They will be born. They will go to schools and a university; they will fall in love. They will find a job. They will grow old and die. But the way of doing these things will be different. Their parents will choose their sex and physical characteristics, and they will be conceived in test tubes. They will have electronic teachers that they only see on TV. They will fall in love through computer dating. They will work at home with a computer hook-up to their jobs. They will grow old with transplanted organs and die when they are 150 years old. Will the world be better? I think there will be less disease, but I think social problems will increase, and war will continue.

```
      PROCESS ──────────────────────▶  IN FUTURE
                                            choose sex
  _____                      _____
          Birth              ╱──▶       _____
        Education            ───▶       _____
  _____           ──▶        _____
  _____           ──▶        _____
      Aging/Death            ──▶        _____
  Overall: _____
           _____
           _____
```

Make a cluster of your own ideas about the future. Are you optimistic or pessimistic? What do you think will happen to humans and to human society?

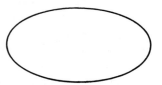

## WRITING

Try to put your ideas into a paragraph. Concentrate on the ideas and the order of the ideas. Don't worry about grammar.

_____

_____

_____

_____

_____

_____

_____

_____

_____

_____

_____

_____

_____

_____

_____

_____

## SHARING

Share your ideas with two of your classmates. What do they think about your predictions? What do you think of theirs? Are there any ideas you would like to change?

## REVISING

Revise the ideas of your paragraph. Add, subtract, reorder; try to present your ideas as effectively as possible.

_____

_____

_____

_____

_____

_____

_____

_____

_____

_____

_____

_____

_____

_____

_____

_____


# EDITING

Use these exercises to think about your own editing.

## Exercise A. *That* clauses

*Directions:* Combine sentences using a clause with the word
**that.**

*Example:* I think. **(that)** Future people will go through the
same cycle of life.

I think that future people will go through the same
cycle of life.

1. I think. **(that)** They will have the same problems as people
of today.

_____

2. I think. **(that)** They will fall in love.

_____

3. I think. **(that)** They will work at home.

_____

4. I think. **(that)** There will be less disease.

_____

5. I think. **(that)** Social problems will increase.

_____

## Exercise B. Punctuation and capitalization

**Directions:** Put in necessary punctuation and capitalization.

what will the world be like in the future i think that future
people will go through the same cycle of life and have the
same problems as people today they will be born they will go
to schools and a university they will fall in love they will find a
job they will grow old and die but the way of doing these things
will be different their parents will choose their sex and physical
characteristics and they will be conceived in test tubes they will
have electronic teachers that they only see on tv they will fall
in love through computer dating they will work at home with a
computer hook-up to their jobs they will grow old with transplanted organs and die when they are 150 years old will the
world be better i think there will be less disease but i think
social problems will increase and war will continue

## Exercise C. Verbs

**Directions:** Fill in the blanks with a verb from the following list.
Make the verbs **future tense.**

| become | fight | be (2) | depend |
| make | change | have (2) | |

I think the world _____ a lot in the future.
                              1

By the year 2100, I believe that the strongest countries

_____ Brazil, Canada, Australia, Zaire, the
         2

Soviet Union, and possibly Greenland. These countries

_____ the most power because of their natural
         3

resources. The industrialized countries of Europe, the United

States, and Japan _____ on these countries for
                              4
the fuel to operate their dying technologies. Despite the pres-

ence of nuclear weapons, I believe that countries still

_____ other countries with guns and bombs. The
          5
Middle East still _____ war as it has for 3000
                          6
years, and, in my opinion, Canada _____ a battle-
                                              7
field because it is between the Soviet Union and the United

States. I have a pessimistic view of the future. I think that sci-

ence _____ the world worse, and that the twenty-
              8
second century _____ the darkest ages of the hu-
                        9
man spirit.

# PARAGRAPH
# 16

*Write about your last three months.*

## PREWRITING

What have you done in the last three months? Has it been a happy, sad, interesting time? Read the following paragraph, and complete the diagram with your class.

I have been in Davis, California, for most of the last three months. During this time, I have done many things. I have visited Old Sacramento. I have skied in the Sierra Mountains and broken my arm, and I have gambled (and lost) a little money in Lake Tahoe casinos. Last month, I spent several days in San Francisco. While I was there, I visited Berkeley and Sausalito. I have visited my younger brother in Los Angeles twice, and last week I had a terrible time in Disneyland. In Davis, I have made many new friends. I have played a lot of tennis, and I have swum almost every day. I have taken many English classes since I have been here, and I have learned a lot of English. I have written many paragraphs in this class.

Now fill in the following diagram.

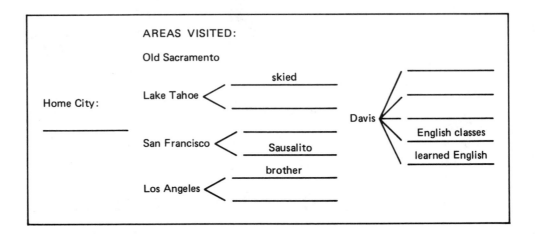

Cluster your last three months. Try to recall interesting people you have met and things you have done.

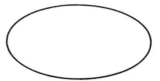

## WRITING

Transform your cluster into a paragraph. Work on communicating your ideas clearly. Try not to worry about grammar at this point.

_____

_____

_____

_____

_____

_____

_____

_____

_____

_____

_____

_____

_____

_____

_____

## SHARING

Exchange paragraphs with three of your classmates. Ask your classmates to circle everything they don't understand. Talk to them about their comments.

## REVISING

Use the ideas gained from your conversations with your classmates to rewrite your paragraph. Make it stronger and clearer.

_____

_____

_____

_____

_____

_____

_____

_____

_____

_____

_____

_____

_____

_____

_____


# EDITING

Use these exercises to help you edit your paragraph.


**Exercise A.** Verbs

>    _Directions:_ Put in the **present perfect** or **past tense,** as
>                  appropriate.

I (be) _____ in the United States since Febru-
                    1

ary. First I (live) _____ in Miami; then I (move)
                         2

_____ here to Indiana two months ago. Since
          3

I (be) _____ in Bloomington, I (visit)
               4

_____ Chicago and Indianapolis. In Chicago, I
          5

(see) _____ a Chicago Bulls' basketball game
             6

one night, and the next day I (go) _____ to the
                                              7

Merchandise Mart. On Memorial Day, my host family (take)

_____ me to the Indianapolis 500 race, and I
          8

(have) _____ a great time. But mostly, I (stay)
               9

_____ in Bloomington. I (go) _____
          10                                              11

to many movies, university plays, and musical concerts. The

weather (be) _____ very humid so far this sum-
                      12

mer, but I like Bloomington very much.

### Exercise B. Prepositions and articles

*Directions:*  Put in **for, in, during, since, of, a, an,** or **the.**

I have been _____ Davis, California, _____ most
                1                                        2

_____ _____ last three months. _____ this time, I
      3           4                                  5

have done many things. I have visited Old Sacramento. I have

skied _____ _____ Sierra Mountains, and I have gam-
             6           7

bled _____ little money _____ Lake Tahoe casinos.
           8                          9

Last month, I spent several days _____ San Francisco.
                                            10

While I was there, I visited Berkeley and Sausalito. I have vis-

ited my brother _____ Los Angeles twice, and last week I
                      11

went to Disneyland. _____ Davis, I have made many new
                         12

friends. I have played _____ lot _____ tennis, and I
                            13              14

have swum almost every day. I have taken many English

classes _____ I have been here, and I have learned
              15

_____ lot _____ English.
      16              17

### Exercise C. Compound sentences

*Directions:*  Study the paragraph on page 104 and Exercise A
                  carefully. Write down the eight compound sen-
                  tences you see.

In the paragraph on page 104:

**1.** _____

_____

**2.** _____

_____

**3.** _____

_____

**4.** _____

_____

In Exercise A:

**5.** _____

_____

**6.** _____

_____

**7.** _____

_____

**8.** _____

_____

# PARAGRAPH
# 17

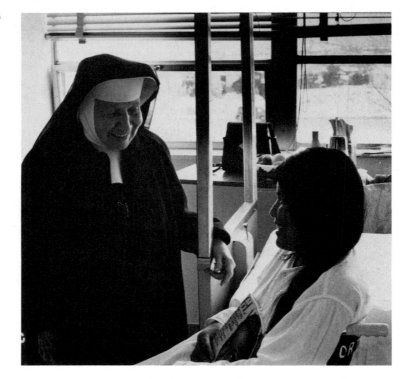

*Write about what makes a good person.*

# PREWRITING

What do you think makes a "good" person? Discuss the following paragraph with your classmates. Do you agree with the writer?

To be well-educated, a person must do five important things. First, she must use her time wisely. She should not watch too much TV, and she should plan her days carefully. Second, she must not limit her studies. She should try to study as many different subjects as she can. For example, if she is a scientist, she should study music, art, and drama. She must see the relationship between different fields. Third, she must have imagination. She must be ready to see what others are unwilling or unable to see. Fourth, she must have self-confidence. She should listen to what others say; however, she must trust herself enough to choose the good from the bad. Fifth, she must never let her curiosity die. She must always look for knowledge, not wait for it to come to her.

## *Questions*

1. The assignment was "Write about what makes a good person." Did the writer follow the assignment? Explain.
2. Do you think that the writer emphasizes the intellectual or emotional aspect of a person? Explain.
3. Do you think that the writer would agree with this statement: "Uneducated people are less likely to be 'good' than educated people"? Do you agree? Explain.
4. Write a one-sentence definition of "good."

You are going to write this paragraph with one of your classmates. Sit together and make a cluster together concerning your ideas. Use your experience and what you have learned from parents, reading, or education to write a "prescription" for being a good person.

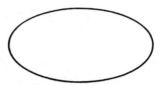

## WRITING

First, write the paragraph by yourself on a piece of paper. Then talk with your classmate and blend your sentences together into one paragraph.

_____
_____
_____
_____
_____
_____
_____
_____
_____

_____

_____

_____

_____

_____

_____

_____

# SHARING

Share your paragraph with another team. Be completely honest. Tell the other team every problem you see in their paragraph.

# REVISING

With your classmate, revise your paragraph. Try to make it clearer.

_____

_____

_____

_____

_____

_____

_____

_____

_____

_____

_____

_____

_____

_____

_____

# EDITING

Go over these exercises with your classmates. See if they give you some ideas for improving your paragraph.

**Exercise A.** Verbs

*Directions:* Put in the correct form of **have to** or **should** and choose the right base verb from this list: **take, speak, concentrate, read, live, produce.**

To learn a foreign language completely, a person

should concentrate on five important things. First, he

_____ in a country in which people use
         1

the language. It is more difficult to study a foreign language

in a person's native country. Second, the student

_____ an organized course of study;
         2

just studying alone is not enough. Third, the student

_____ on vocabulary and grammar in the class-
         3

room because they are the bases of the language. Fourth, the

student _____ newspapers, magazines, and
         4

books in the language every day, so he can see the language

in real situations. Fifth, the student _____ the
         5

language every day with native speakers, and listen to

native speakers on TV and radio every day. These steps

_____ a knowledge of the language, if the stu-
                  6

dent works hard.

## Exercise B.  Transitions

> ***Directions:***   Look back at the paragraph about being well-
> educated and at the sentences in Exercise B
> about learning a foreign language. Take out the
> words **first, second, third, fourth,** and **fifth.**
> Read the paragraph again and substitute **to begin
> with, next, also, in addition,** and **finally.**

## Exercise C.  Punctuation and capitalization

> ***Directions:***   Put in necessary punctuation and capitalization.

to be well educated a person must do five important things
first she must use her time wisely she should not watch too
much tv and she should plan her days carefully second she
must not limit her studies she should try to study as many different subjects as she can for example if she is a scientist she
should study music art and drama she must see the relationship between different fields third she must have imagination
she must be ready to see what others are unwilling or unable
to see fourth she must have self confidence she should listen
to what others say however she must trust herself enough to
choose the good from the bad fifth she must never let her curiosity die she must always look for knowledge not wait for it to
come to her

# PARAGRAPH
# 18

*Write about
your country.*

## PREWRITING

Read the following paragraph and complete the diagram. Discuss the paragraph and diagram with your class.

A visitor to my country, Qatar, should visit three towns to get a taste of the country. Traveling from south to north, the traveler should first stop at Qatar's main oil terminal, Umm Said. Umm Said is mainly an industrial town with shops, supermarkets, and a golf course for its industrial workers. After he has seen the terminal, the traveler should drive north towards Doha. He will see miles of sandy beaches as he drives along the coast through Wakra, which was once Qatar's most important fishing and pearling village. When he arrives at the capital city of Doha, he will find a large city; eight of every ten Qataris live in Doha. The visitor should walk down the narrow streets of the souq to see the ancient trading markets and the people, and he should visit the Qatar National Museum to learn about the country's history. If the visitor goes to Umm Said, Wakra, and Doha, he should get a good picture of the old and new Qatar.

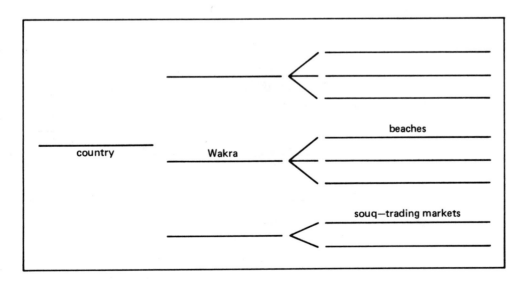

Imagine that you are a tour guide in your country. What places should a tourist see in order to get a complete picture of your country? Make a cluster of your ideas.

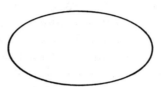

## WRITING

Exchange your cluster with a classmate. Write a paragraph based on your classmate's cluster.

_____

_____

_____

_____

_____

_____

_____

_____
_____
_____
_____
_____
_____
_____
_____
_____
_____

## SHARING

Return the paragraph to the student whose cluster you used. Check the paragraph your classmate wrote on the basis of your cluster. What information did he or she leave out? Is there anything incorrect?

## REVISING

Revise the paragraph about your country completely. Make the communication clear.

_____
_____
_____
_____
_____
_____
_____
_____
_____
_____

_____

_____

_____

_____

_____

_____

_____

# EDITING

Use these exercises to help you edit your paragraph.

**Exercise A.**  Prepositions and articles

_Directions:_  Fill in the blanks, or leave them empty if required.

_____ visitor _____ Israel should visit three important
        1              2

places. Traveling _____ north _____ south, he should go
                    3              4

_____ Lake Kinneret. _____ Kinneret is _____ beautiful,
   5                      6                    7

fresh-water lake surrounded _____ cool, green hills and for-
                              8

ests. After he drives through _____ modern city _____ Tel-
                                9                    10

Aviv, _____ visitor enters _____ desert climate as he nears
        11                     12

Jerusalem. While he is _____ Jerusalem, he should mainly
                         13

visit _____ old city, where he will see Moslems, Christians,
        14

and Jews living _____ an area thousands of years old. He
                  15

should shop _____ the Arabic market near _____ Damascus
              16                              17

Gate, and he should visit _____ Mosque _____ Omar,
                            18            19

_____ Via Dolorosa, and _____ Wailing Wall. After he stays
   20                       21

_____ Jerusalem _____ a few days, he should drive through
   22            23

_____ desert _____ the Dead Sea where he can climb
   24        25

Masada. If the visitor sees _____ Kinneret, Jerusalem, and
                         26

_____ Dead Sea, he should get _____ interesting look
   27                     28

_____ my country.
   29

## Exercise B. Subordinate clauses

*Directions:* Make complex sentences.

1. **(After)** He has seen the oil terminal. The traveler should drive north toward Doha.

   _____

2. **(When)** He arrives in Doha. He will find a large city.

   _____

3. **(After)** He leaves Tel-Aviv. The visitor enters a desert climate.

   _____

4. **(While)** He is in Jerusalem. He should visit the old city.

   _____

## Exercise C. Adjectives

*Directions:* Put an adjective in each blank to make the sentence more descriptive.

1. Umm Said is mainly an industrial town with _____ shops, _____ supermarkets, and a _____ golf course for its industrial workers.

2. He will see miles of _____ white beaches as he drives along the _____ coast.

3. After he has seen the _____ terminal, the traveler should drive north towards Doha.

4. He should shop in the _____ Arabic market.

5. After he stays in Jerusalem for a few days, he should drive through the _____ desert to the Dead Sea.

6. If the visitor sees the _____ Kinneret, _____ Jerusalem, and the _____ Dead Sea, he should get an interesting look at my country.

# PARAGRAPH
# 19

*Write about the person you want to marry.*

## PREWRITING

What kind of person would you like to marry? What characteristics are important to you in a spouse? Read and discuss this paragraph with your class.

I want to get married to another Peruvian when I am 24 years old. Now I will describe the kind of man I want to marry. First, he should come from a good Peruvian family. Second, he should be about two years older than I, about 26. Third, he must look good. I want him to have black hair and a big body. Fourth, he should be smart. He must have a university education. Fifth, I hope he will have a good job in a big city. For example, I would like to marry a doctor in Lima. Sixth, and most important, he must have a kind personality. I think this kind of man will make a good husband and a good father.

Now complete the following diagram.

```
1. Good family

2. Age = _____

                                              black hair
3. _____   <  _____

4. _____   =  university education

5. _____Occupation_____   =  _____

6. _____
```

Think about the kind of person you want to marry. Try to think about five or six important characteristics you are looking for. Make a cluster about your ideal spouse. (If you are already married, make a cluster of the characteristics you admire in your spouse.)

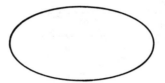

## **WRITING**

Write a paragraph based on your cluster. Try to concentrate on your ideas; don't worry about grammar at this point.

_____

_____

_____

_____

_____

_____

_____

_____

_____

_____

_____

_____

_____

_____

_____

_____

## SHARING

Read your paragraph to a classmate. What does your classmate think about it? Work on the communication of ideas.
Are all your ideas present? Have they been communicated
clearly?

## REVISING

Revise your paragraph. When you are satisfied, give the
paragraph to your classmate, and obtain your classmate's
paragraph. Revise this paragraph also, changing whatever
you like. Compare your revisions with your classmate's.

_____

_____

_____

_____

_____

_____

_____

_____

_____

_____

_____

_____

_____

_____

_____

_____

Revision of classmate's paragraph:

_____

_____

_____

_____

_____

_____

_____

_____

_____

_____

_____

_____

_____

_____

_____

_____

# EDITING

Use these exercises to help you in editing your paragraph.

### Exercise A.  Articles

*Directions:*  Put in **a, an, the,** or leave the space blank.

I think _____ right age for me to get married is 28. I want to
        <sub>1</sub>

marry _____ woman who is about 23. First, she should have
    <sub>2</sub>

_____ good personality. I want _____ wife who is _____ sweet
 <sub>3</sub>             <sub>4</sub>          <sub>5</sub>

and kind to children. Second, she should be _____ intelligent. I
                <sub>6</sub>

don't care if she has _____ university degree, but I want her to
          <sub>7</sub>

have _____ open mind. Third, I want her to be _____ beautiful
   <sub>8</sub>                     <sub>9</sub>

woman. She should be _____ little shorter than I, and I hope
          <sub>10</sub>

she will have _____ brown hair and _____ green eyes. I'm
      <sub>11</sub>           <sub>12</sub>

sure my future wife will not be like _____ woman I have de-
             <sub>13</sub>

scribed, but I hope so!

### Exercise B.  Relative clauses

*Directions:*  Change the second sentence to a relative clause,
and put it inside the first sentence.

*Example:*  I will choose a man. He will be about five years older
than I. **(who)**
I will choose a man who will be about five years
older than I.

1.  I want a wife. She will be kind to children. **(that)**

_____

**2.** I want a husband. He will like to work around the house.
**(who)**

_____

**3.** My husband will be a smart man. He has a college degree.
**(who)**

_____

**4.** My future wife will be from my city. This city is in Turkey.
**(which)**

_____

## Exercise C.  Punctuation and capitalization

**Directions:**  Put in the necessary punctuation and capitalization.

i want to get married to another peruvian when i am 24 years old now i will describe the kind of man i want to marry first he should come from a good peruvian family second he should be about two years older than i about 26 third he must look good i want him to have black hair and a big body fourth he should be smart he must have a university education fifth i hope he will have a good job in a big city for example i would like to marry a doctor in lima sixth and most important he must have a kind personality i think this kind of man will make a good husband and a good father

# PARAGRAPH
# 20

*Write about your life*
*at age 75.*

# PREWRITING

Can you imagine life at age 75? What will it be like? Read and discuss the following paragraph with your class.

When I am 75 years old, I would like to be healthy, to live comfortably, and to have a nice family. I would not like to be like many old people. I hope that I will stay in good condition because I would like to swim, jog, and play tennis regularly. Also I would like to have enough money to live easily, not too much and not too little. I would like to have a large house on the beach and a nice car. I hope that I will not have to live on money from the government or from my children. Most important, I'd like to have a good family with three or four grandchildren to play with. I'd like to have a good reputation, with the respect of myself and the people who know me.

What are four things the writer of this paragraph is afraid of?

1. _____
2. _____
3. _____
4. _____

How much money do you think the writer believes is "enough money to live easily"?

What do you think the writer believes is "a nice car"?

What do you think the writer believes is "a good family"?

Cluster your own desires about life at age 75. What ideas come to mind? What kind of life do you want?

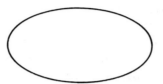

## WRITING

Use your cluster to write a paragraph. Remember: clear ideas, clear communication. Make changes as you write, if you wish.

_____

_____

_____

_____

_____

_____

_____

_____

_____

_____

_____

_____

_____

_____

_____

_____

## SHARING

Read your paragraph to the entire class, and ask for comments. Is there anything you left out? Is there anything your classmates don't understand?

## REVISING

Rewrite your paragraph, making it stronger and clearer. Make as many changes as you want.

_____

_____

_____

_____

_____

_____

_____

_____

_____

_____

_____

_____

_____

_____

_____

_____

## EDITING

Edit your paragraph after completing these exercises.

### Exercise A. Verbs

**Directions:** Change the verb from **would like** to **hope that** plus the **future tense.**

**Example:** I would not like to live like many old people.
I hope that I will not live like many old people.

1. I would like to be able to swim.

_____

2. I would like to have enough money to live easily.

_____

3. I would like to have a nice family.

_____

4. I would like to have a good reputation.

_____

### Exercise B. Punctuation and capitalization

**Directions:** Put in the necessary punctuation and capitalization.

when i am 75 years old i would like to be healthy to live

comfortably and to have a nice family i would not like to be like

many old people i hope that i will stay in good condition because i would like to swim jog and play tennis regularly also i
would like to have enough money to live easily not too much
and not too little i would like to have a large house on the
beach and a nice car i hope that i will not have to live on
money from the government or from my children most important i'd like to have a good family with three or four grandchildren to play with i'd like to have a good reputation with the
respect of myself and the people who know me

## Exercise C.  Infinitives

*Directions:*   From the list below, choose an infinitive to put into
each sentence.

| | | |
|---|---|---|
| to have | to get | to play |
| to spend | to lead | to go |
| to watch | to drink | to meet |
| to visit | | |

At this time of my life, I would like _____ most of
$\overline{1}$
my time with my friends and family in my native Toledo. In the

mornings, I'd like _____ up at 5:00 A.M. Then I would
$\overline{2}$

like _____ a cup of strong coffee, and read and write
$\overline{3}$

for a few hours before I go to oversee my vineyards. Like my

grandfathers before me, I would like _____ to the
$\overline{4}$

bullfights on summer afternoons. Afterwards, I would like

_____ my friends in our favorite cafe, and I would like
$\overline{5}$

_____ cards, dominoes, and chess with them. And I
$\overline{6}$

would like _____ the beautiful Toledan sunsets with a
$\overline{7}$

glass of my vineyard's red wine in my hand and my family

at my side. In the evenings, I'd like ＿＿＿＿＿ friends
                                              8

and have them visit me. Then at 10:00 P.M., I would like

＿＿＿＿＿ a big dinner with my family, smoke a cigar, and
        9

drink a little sherry. I hope that I will be able ＿＿＿＿＿
                                                       10

this kind of life, and I think that I will.